The SCIENCE of

F·U·N·S·T·A·T·I·O·N

POWER

GODFREY HALL

FUNSTATION is an exciting new combination of information
and equipment designed to educate and entertain.

With over 100 colour illustrations packed into 48 pages and
additional cut out and press out cards and stickers at the
back of the book your FUNSTATION provides a
comprehensive introduction to the exciting world of Science.

A DESIGN EYE BOOK

First published in 1995 by Design Eye Ltd
4-6 Dunmow Road, Bishop's Stortford,
Hertfordshire CM23 5HL, United Kingdom

ISBN 1 872700 39 X

The Design Eye Team

Michael Tout
Lee Robinson
Aline Serra Littlejohn
Sally Symes
Joanne Coles

With thanks to our contributors
Mary Budd and Janet Swarbrick.
Illustrations by Peter Serjeant.
Cover illustration by Janos Marffy.

3 5 7 9 10 8 6 4

Manufactured in China

WARNING! Non-rechargeable batteries are not to be recharged. Rechargeable batteries are to be removed before recharging. Rechargeable batteries are only to be recharged under adult supervision. Do not mix old and new batteries or alkaline, standard (carbon-zinc) or rechargeable (nickel-cadmium) batteries. Only use batteries of the same or equivalent type. Batteries are to be inserted with the correct polarity. Exhausted batteries are to be removed. Supply terminals must not be short-circuited.

Contents

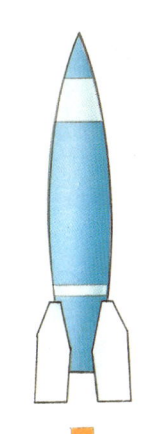

INTRODUCTION

For anything in your home to move and work it needs energy to give it power. Even before prehistoric man tried to make fire by rubbing two stones together people had been working out how to make their own power. Later on, people first used the natural power of wind and water to turn windmill sails and waterwheels to power other machinery. Today the energy of moving air or water is used to generate electricity that powers machines.

Scientists also investigate energy such as heat, light, sound, nuclear, electrical, solar and chemical energy from fuels like petrol and gas. Power sources may be as simple as the natural muscle power of a snail, or the wind-blown sail of a toy yacht; or as complex as the electrically powered Eurostar train that travels at speeds of well over 200 kph, or the complex engine of a jet-propelled aircraft.

Your Funstation will help you experiment to find out more about how and why things move and work, and how to produce your own power.

BEFORE YOU START

- It is important to have plenty of space for your experiments. Some can be done on the floor or the kitchen table or, if the weather is fine, on an open flat space outside.
- Make sure that you cover any surface with plenty of newspaper before you start.
- Look for the safety triangle. ⚠ This sign in the margin by the experiment means that extra care is needed. You must ask an adult to help you with it.
- Most of the things you will need for your experiments are contained in this pack or can be found around your home.
- Always ask before you borrow something.
- Always clear up everything when you have finished.

WHAT NEXT?

This section of each page will provide you with suggestions of other ideas you might like to try out connected with the topic. If you have made a model you may want to change the design to improve the way it works. If the experiment hasn't worked very well you may want to have another go.

Visit your local library for some more books on the subjects or talk to your teacher at school about what you have been doing.

WHAT MAKES A GOOD SCIENTIST?

- Make sure that you have collected together all you need before you start on any experiment.
- Before you start on an experiment jot down in your Funstation notebook (at the back) what you think might happen.
- Keep the equipment you use for your experiments separate from the ordinary pots and pans used by the family.
- Don't worry if your experiment doesn't work the first time. Often you will have to try something out two or three times to get a good result.
- Write down what happens in each step in your notebook. It is sometimes quite difficult to remember afterwards what actually happened a few minutes before. If you want to try the experiment again it is useful to know what has happened before.
- Write down your results in your notebook. After your experiment ask yourself some of these questions. Did it work as it said in the book. If not, why not? Try it again. You may not have followed the instructions correctly or you may have used the wrong things.

TAKE CARE

It is very important to make sure that everything you do is completely safe. If the safety triangle ⚠ tells you that you will need an adult's help be sure to ask someone before you start.
- Put on an apron or overall before you start.
- Be careful with any sharp tools such as scissors or screwdrivers.
- Wash your hands after you have finished an experiment.
- Always ask for help from an adult if you are not sure about anything.
- Never play with electrical equipment or near a socket. Electricity can be very dangerous and could kill you.
- Never use anything hot without asking for an adult's help.

MOVE IT!

Once the wheel was invented, 5,000 years ago, people no longer had to drag or push things along the ground. Things really started moving! The first wheels were made of solid wood so the ride was uncomfortable and bumpy. Today's air-filled rubber tyres give a smoother ride.

WONDER WHEELS

Wheels are extremely useful machines especially as they can be joined onto other machines to increase their power. They are particularly useful for our everyday transport of bicycles, cars, buses and trains.

Make a collection of objects that might be used as wheels. These could include cotton reels, lids, construction kit wheels, or wooden wheels from old toys. See if you can divide them into different sizes. Keep them safe as they may be useful later in the book.

AXLE POWER

The axle is the bar to which a wheel is fixed. An axle like that on a wheelbarrow may have only one wheel. But the advantage of an axle is that it can have a wheel at either end, so enabling two wheels to turn round at the same time. You can make an axle out of a length of dowelling rod, wire or a straw.

If you use wire it is a good idea to bend the end of the wire into a loop so it fits back into the middle of the wheel to stop it falling off. The wheel moves more freely on a wire axle. It is important to remember this when you are making a model.

Try fixing your wheels to dowelling, wire or a straw. Which works the best?

MAKE YOUR OWN RACING CAR

You will need • 4 plastic cotton reels • 2 pieces of dowelling or 2 straws for axles • 2 bulldog clips • a short ruler • plasticine • racing car template at the back of the book • sticky tape

1 Trace your car template onto card and colour and cut out two car shapes. Tape one on each side of the ruler.

2 Fix the bulldog clips to the ruler as shown. Push the two dowelling rods or straws through the clips.

3 Fix on the plastic cotton reels. Put a piece of plasticine at the end of each of the axles to stop the cotton reels falling off. See how far your buggy will move with a gentle push.

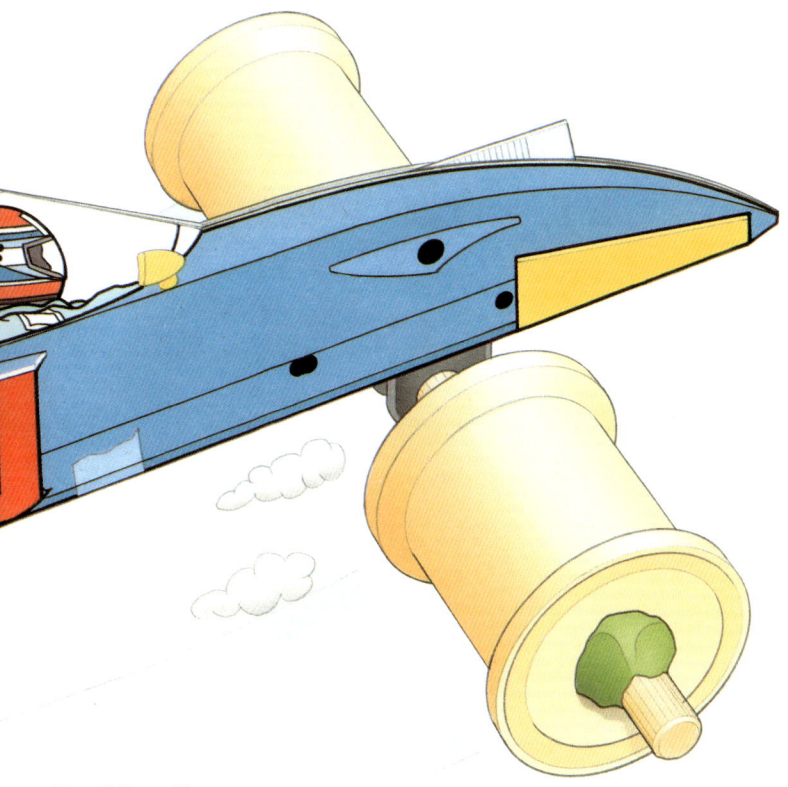

DID YOU KNOW?
Big 300-tonne caterpillar trucks that move earth have tyres which cost thousands of pounds each.

LAND RACERS

Land yacht racing is becoming a very popular sport. You can often see the racers with their brightly coloured sails "land sailing" over long stretches of sandy beach. These special craft are designed to use the power of the wind. They have large sails to catch the wind and wheels that will move easily across the sand.

Not only has wind power been used to move huge boats with sails, like those of the Spanish Armada, it is also used to move windmill sails to drive machinery inside the windmills.

MAKE A LAND RACER
You will need • card vehicle templates from the back of the book • sticky tape • 2 straws • 4 cotton reels • scissors • coloured pens

1 Make your vehicle using the instructions at the back of the book.

2 Thread a straw axle through each of the holes in the axle holders 1 and 2. Thread your second straw through the holes in 3 and 4.

3 Fix a cotton reel to the end of each axle. Attach a piece of plasticine to the ends of the straw axles to stop the cotton reels falling off.

FITTING THE SAIL
You will need • the sail template and stickers from the back of the book • 1 straw • a pencil • scissors • thin card or paper

1 Draw round the sail template and transfer it onto thin card or paper. Decorate it using your stickers. Cut it out and cut two holes in your sail as shown.

2 Thread the straw through the two holes in the sail.

3 Carefully push the straw a little way through the hole in the bottom of the vehicle. You may need to tape the straw to keep it securely in place.

WHAT NEXT?

• Take your land racer outside and see if the wind will move it. If not then ask an adult to provide some air using a hair dryer.

HOW IT WORKS

The force of the wind will push against the sail and move your racer. The wheels you have fitted will help make it move smoothly.

GEAR WHEELS

Gears are toothed wheels which link together in pairs so that one turns the other. They can change the speed and force of other wheels. They can be found in all kinds of machines from the tiny ones in a watch which move the hands, in rotary egg whisks, clocks and bicycles, to cars and complicated industrial machines.

Gears of different sizes turn at different speeds. They can be used to make a wheel move in a different direction or to make it easier to cycle up a hill. The gears of a car help when it is starting off by allowing the engine to turn quickly while the wheels turn slowly, and they enable the car to gain speed or slow down.

GETTING TO GRIPS
You will need • 3 different-sized cogwheels from the back of the book • a piece of card • 3 paper fasteners

1 Push a paper fastener through the middle of a gear wheel from the back of the book and through the piece of card. Spread out the tails of the fastener at the back of the cardboard to keep the cogwheel in place on the card but so that you can turn the cogwheel.

2 Fit the second cogwheel in the same way so that the cogs link with the first wheel.

3 The third wheel you fit onto the card must only link with one of the other wheels. If all three touch they will jam.

WHAT NEXT?
• Record in your notebook how many times each cogwheel goes round compared with another. Record your results.

DID YOU KNOW?
Racing bicycles with up to 20 gears enable cyclists to maintain speed up very steep hills.

In 1885 J. K. Starley invented a bicycle with gears and solid rubber wheels both the same size – different to earlier versions like the Penny Farthing and the Boneshaker!

BOTTLE TOP COGWHEELS

Collect some metal bottle tops with a wavy edge.

⚠ **1** Ask an adult to make a hole with a nail through the middle of each top.

⚠ **2** Fit the tops together on the wooden board and ask the adult to help you nail each top onto the board so they all link together, and when you move the first one the others will move.

Can you find any other things that could be used to make gears?

HOW IT WORKS

You will notice that the smaller the wheel the more times it has to turn compared with the bigger wheel.

Gears have to be made of very strong material as each cog on each wheel gets a lot of use.

ON YOUR BIKE

• Take a look at your bicycle. Lift the back wheel off the floor. Turn the pedals once to make one turn of the chain wheel. Do this again, but this time count the number of times the back wheel turns. Record your results in your notebook.

If your bicycle has a set of gears see what difference each gear makes to the number of turns of the wheel. Make a record of your results.

FUN WITH BOATS

One of the first boats was probably a simple log. Used by very early hunters it would have been just right for fishing in a river or going to visit friends further down stream!

Today some boats carry very heavy loads of goods, whether bananas or motor cars, thousands of miles around the world.

Although modern ships are built of steel there are still many that are made of wood. Boats can be powered by the wind, by paddles or by motors. Use your Funstation boat to try out some of these ideas.

WIND IN YOUR SAILS

The wind can be used to move a boat easily across the water.

You will need • your Funstation boat • boat propellors and mast • the sail template from the back of the book • water

Trace round your sail template onto paper. Cut it out and fit it onto the mast provided. Fix it to the base of the boat. Try several different-shaped sails and see which works the best.

MATCHSTICK POWER

You will need • 2 dead matches • a sliver of soap • a pinch of washing powder • water

Split the end of a dead match. Place the piece of soap on or in between the split. Put your match boat in the water. The boat will move. Now try a pinch of washing powder.

HOW IT WORKS

The soap weakens the surface tension of the water under it. Because the tension is now stronger at the other end of the boat it moves forward.

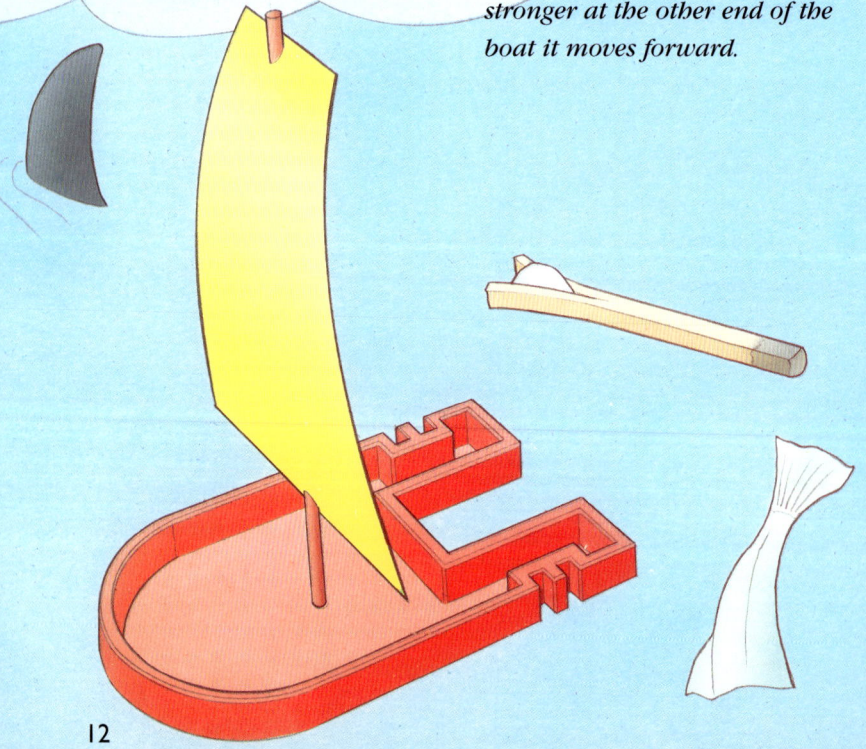

PADDLE POWER

You will need • your Funstation boat • 2 paddle blades from your Funstation pack • a rubber band • water

One simple way of powering your boat is to use paddles. Take the two paddle blades in the pack and fit them together to make a paddle as illustrated. Fit the rubber band around the paddle blades. Fix it over the slots at the back of the boat. Put some water in a washing-up bowl or a sink.

Twist the rubber band round several times. Hold it in place. Put your boat in the water. Let it go. It should move quickly through the water.

What happens if you wind the rubber band the other way?

MAKE YOUR OWN HOVERCRAFT

You will need • a small cardboard lid • a cardboard tube • scissors

Trace a circle round the end of the cardboard tube in the middle of the lid. Cut out the circle to make a hole in the middle of the cardboard lid. Fix the cardboard tube into this hole. Blow down the tube and watch what happens.

HOW IT WORKS

The air you blow down the cardboard tube makes a cushion of air under the lid which causes it to rise.

The hovercraft that cross the English Channel work in the same way. The huge rubber "skirt" under the craft fills with pressurised air. This air cushion enables the hovercraft to travel smoothly over snow, ice and even swamps.

WHAT NEXT?

• Can you think of some other ways of powering your boat? You could try fitting a blown-up balloon onto the craft and then letting go. What would happen? Once you let go will the boat shoot across the water?

PUSH AND PULL!

For thousands of years, long before the wheel was invented, simple levers and pulleys were used to move large and heavy weights like the huge boulders and rocks of the Pyramids and Stonehenge.

To move a stone out of the way you might put a long stick under it and push down on the other end of the stick. When doing this you are in fact using a lever.

It needs less effort to use a lever than to push something with your hands, and pulleys are useful for lifting heavy objects up vertically with little effort. The more pulleys used together the less effort will be needed.

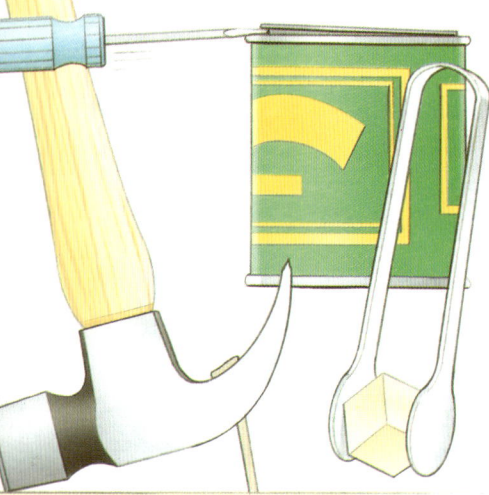

LEVERS AT WORK

There are three types of lever. For example, a spoon used to push a lid off a tin, or a clawhammer used to push a nail out of wood are class one levers. When you crack a nut with a pair of nutcrackers you are using a second class lever. When you use sugar tongs to pick up a lump of sugar you are using a third class lever.

HAUL AWAY!

Make a lifting lever.

You will need • a strip of thick card 26 cm long and 4 cm wide • scissors • marbles • a small cardboard box • strong cord or string • a wooden board • a drawing pin

1 Pin the card strip to the wooden board as shown.

2 Tie one end of string to one end of the strip. Tape the box to the other end of string.

3 Pull down the free end of the lever to lift the box. Record how many marbles your lever will lift before it bends.

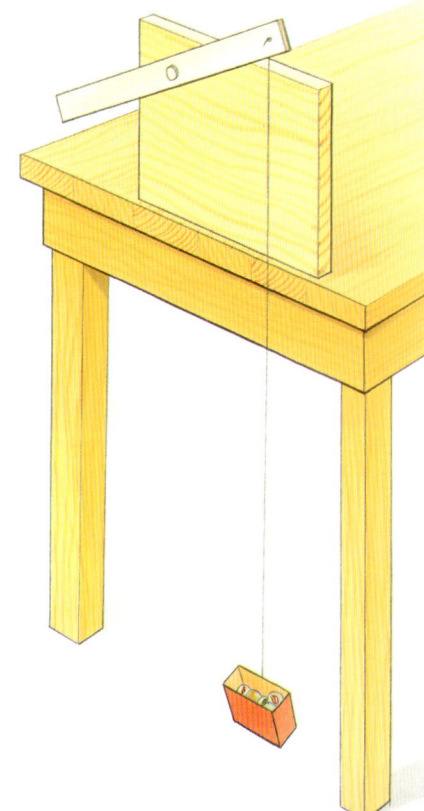

PULLEYS AT WORK

You will need • a piece of wood about 45 cm long and 30cm wide • marbles • a small cardboard box • strong cord or string • a wooden board • a drawing pin • building blocks or books

Build up one end of your piece of wood with blocks or books to make a slope.

1 Tie the cardboard box to the string and drop it over the top end of the slope. Add some marbles to the box.

2 Hold the other end of the string and pull the box upwards.

3 Now fit the cardboard tube under the string at the top end of the slope. Does this make it any easier to pull the box?

4 Now try the plastic cotton reel. When you pull the string over it does it feel smoother than over the tube? Why is this?

How It Works

There is less friction between the string and the smoother plastic surface, so this should be easier to use than cardboard.

A Simple Pulley

⚠ **1** Use one of the pulley wheels from your Funstation kit. Ask an adult to help you fix the wheel to a piece of wood with a pin or tacking nail.

2 Make sure that you put a bead from your kit between the wood and the pulley. This will make it turn more easily.

3 Loop a piece of string over the pulley and fix a weight on the other end. Pull the string and raise the weight.

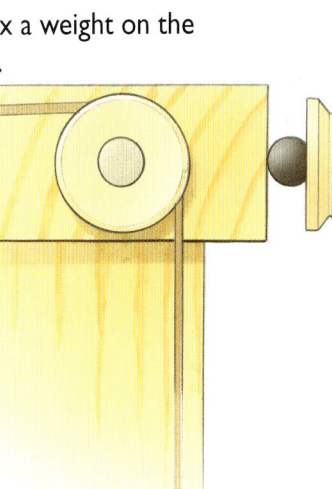

How It Works

Pulleys let you move heavy weights with very little force. You may have to pull the string a long way downwards for the weight to move a short way upwards. Try two pulleys together to make lifting even easier.

Did You Know?

Cranes are pulleys that are used to lift huge containers onto ships, and pulleys are also used to move ski lifts.

IN A SPIN!

A spin dryer machine is very useful for drying the washing. It uses a centrifugal force that pushes outwards on the water moving in a circle. Twin-tub washing machines have a spin dryer tub separate from the wash tub but most modern day washing machines have a spin dryer as part of the washing tub. Here is a simple spin dryer that you can make and then test.

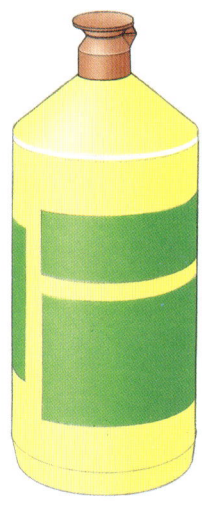

You will need • a string about 30 cm long • a shorter string about 16 cm long • a clean empty plastic bottle • a wet cloth • scissors • a plastic cotton reel • a dowelling rod

⚠ **1** Cut the top off the plastic bottle. In the bottom part make a small hole each side near the top as shown. Tie the short string through the holes to make a handle. Carefully make more holes in the sides as shown.

2 Tie the long string to the handle as shown. Push the end of the string through the middle of the cotton reel and tie the string to the doweling rod.

3 With the wet cloth in the dryer hold the cotton reel with the spin dryer hanging below it. Spin the rod around fast. As the dryer spins so the water comes out through the holes in the sides.

HOW IT WORKS

As the spin dryer rotates the centrifugal force pushes the water to the sides and it escapes through the holes. This is how a real spin dryer works but at a very much higher speed. As it spins round at high speed all the water is pushed to the sides and drawn out of the dryer.

DID YOU KNOW?

At the fairground some of the rides, many looking like big cylinders, use centrifugal force. As the ride spins round so the people are pushed to the sides and look as though they are stuck to the walls. Many people find this great fun!

WHAT NEXT?

• Take your dryer outside and spin it round your head on the end of the string. See if the piece of cloth is drier than before. Another way to make your dryer work is to tie the string to the end of a ⚠ hand drill. As you turn the drill the dryer spins round.

MAGNET POWER

Around every magnet is a "magnetic field" where the magnet can exert its powers to push or pull. Scientists are still investigating this invisible force.

One end of a magnet always turns to point north. That end is called the north pole, the other end is the south pole. Place two magnets together so the two opposite poles are facing each other, and you will notice that they are drawn together. Place the same poles (north with north or south with south) together and they will swing away from, or repel each other.

MOVING MAGNETS

You can use the power of the magnets to move things.

You will need • your Funstation vehicle • 2 bar magnets • strong sticky tape • a piece of wood about 45 cm long and 30cm wide • building blocks or books

1 Fix one of the bar magnets to your Funstation vehicle as shown with strong sticky tape.

2 Put the vehicle on the floor. Hold the other bar magnet pointing towards the first magnet. Move it towards the vehicle and if it moves away from you turn your magnet round. You should be able to pull the vehicle along the ground. This is using the magnetic force of the two magnets and they do not need to touch.

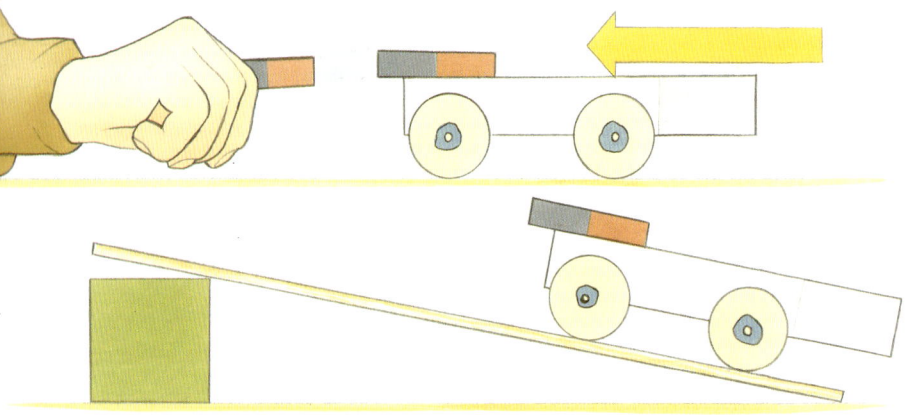

3 Build up one end of your piece of wood with blocks or books to make a gentle slope. Put your buggy at the bottom of the slope and see if you can pull it upwards using the other magnet.

WHAT NEXT?

• Increase the number of blocks or books to make your slope steeper. How steep must your slope be before the magnetic pull of your magnet stops working? Record your results in your notebook.

MAGNETIC BOAT RACE

Magnets can also move things across water.

You will need • 2 corks • 2 metal paper clips • 2 long pins • 2 bar magnets or one bar and a horseshoe magnet • 2 sticks 30cm long • a large washing up bowl • strong sticky tape • sail stickers from the back of the book • scissors •

1 Unbend one end of a metal paper clip and fix it into a cork as illustrated.

2 Push the pin into the cork as shown.

3 Carefully fold one of your sail stickers around the pin as shown. Then make up your second boat in the same way.

4 Tape a bar magnet to the end of a stick. Alternatively, use your horseshoe magnet for this experiment.

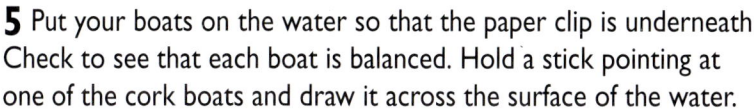

5 Put your boats on the water so that the paper clip is underneath. Check to see that each boat is balanced. Hold a stick pointing at one of the cork boats and draw it across the surface of the water.

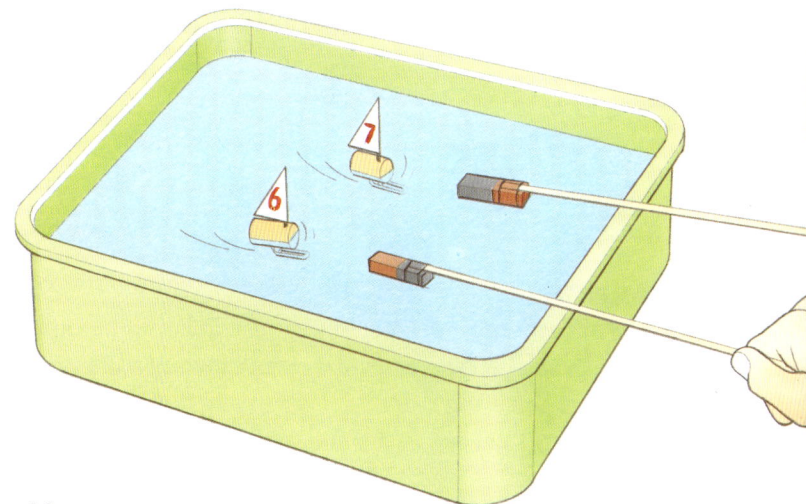

WHAT NEXT?

• Create your own races across the bowl. Make some markers using other corks and make your own race circuit. Try out different sails to see if they make any difference to the speed of your cork boat.

DID YOU KNOW?

Japanese Magalev trains use their magnetic field to float above their tracks. With no moving parts, the trains are very light and environmentally friendly. One train travelled at over 500 kph!

Pulling Power

How much effort do you need to pull a weight up a slope? Does it make any difference if the slope is gentle or steep? Though you may need to travel further on a gentle slope the effort required to pull the weight up will be much less than pulling the weight up the shorter distance of a steep slope.

Up The Ramp

You will need • a piece of wood about 45 cm long and 30cm wide • building blocks or books • your Funstation or a toy vehicle • a long piece of string

1 Build up one end of your piece of wood with one block or book to make a gentle slope. Tie the string to the end of your vehicle and pull it up the slope.

2 Pile up two more blocks or books to make a steeper slope. Is it more difficult to pull the vehicle up the slope?

3 Pulling the car gets harder as the slope is increased.

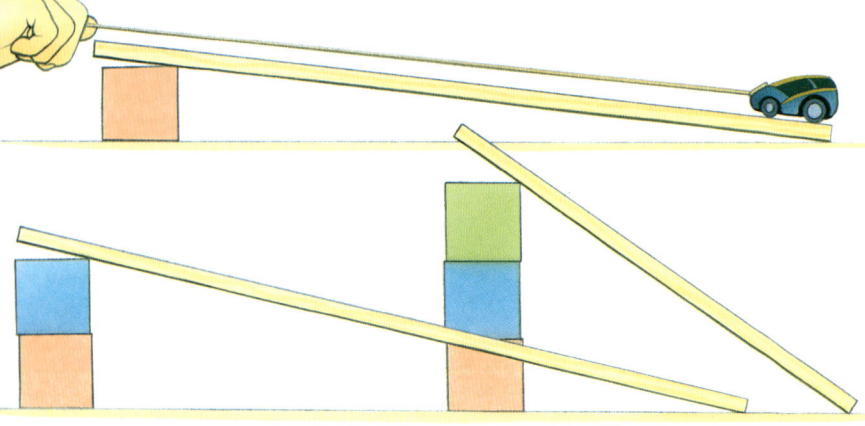

What Next?

• See what happens if you keep the same number of blocks or books but make the slope shorter. Find a piece of wood half the length of your original piece and record the difference it makes to the amount of effort needed to pull the vehicle up the slope.

How It Works

As the slope increases so it gets harder to pull things up it. Many new shopping malls have winding slopes that are much easier to climb. This idea is used on roads that climb mountains. It is easier to walk up a mountain by taking the winding road than trying to walk straight up the mountain-side which would require an enormous amount of effort. The winding road is acting as a simple machine. It increases the distance you move in order to decrease the effort you must use to reach the top of the mountain.

RUBBER BAND STRETCH

You will need • a thick rubber band • a heavy weight • a piece of wood about 45 cm long and 30cm wide • building blocks or books • a long piece of string • ruler, pencil and paper (for measuring and recording)

1 Build up one end of your piece of wood with blocks or books to make a gentle slope.

2 Measure and record the length of your rubber band.

3 Tie the string around the weight and then tie the other end to the rubber band.

4 Use the rubber band to pull the weight up the slope. Stop half way up the slope and get someone to measure and record the new length of the rubber band. How much has the rubber band stretched? Record your results in your notebook.

5 Now put the weight on the floor and lift it using the rubber band. Get someone to measure and record the length of the rubber band. Is the rubber band stretched further when you use the slope or when you lift the weight from the floor?

HOW IT WORKS

The longer the rubber band, the more force you need to move the weight. The difference in length shows that you need a lot less force to move the weight up the slope.

WHAT NEXT?

• Can you find examples in your local area where spirals and slopes are used instead of steep inclines?

DID YOU KNOW?

Force is measured in newtons after Sir Isaac Newton, one of our greatest scientists. The laws of motion he developed in 1665–66 are still in use today. He also discovered the law of gravity and that white light is made up of many colours.

Jet Propelled!

The earliest engine of 1712 was powered simply by steam and was used to pump water. In 1765 James Watts built a steam engine six times more powerful, and in 1814 George Stephenson built a steam locomotive called The Rocket. Later engines used coal, gas and air as fuel, and petrol and diesel engines were developed. In 1929 Frank Whittle designed the first jet engine and the first jet plane flew in 1941. Today many engines are driven by electricity.

The most powerful engine is the rocket which can lift a heavy spacecraft off the ground and send it into space.

Jet Propulsion

You will need • strong thread about 1 1/2 m long • two chairs • the long sausage balloon • a plastic straw • sticky tape

1 Feed a strong thread through a plastic straw. Stretch the thread between two chairs and fix each end to a chair. Make sure the thread is tight and taut.

2 Blow up the balloon and hold the end so that the air cannot escape. Or you could use a clip or some sticky tape.

3 Get someone to help you fix the balloon underneath the straw with sticky tape. Be careful not to let the air out of the balloon.

4 Push the balloon on the straw to one end of the thread. It must move easily along the thread. Let go of the balloon and watch what happens. It should rush along the thread at high speed!

How It Works

The air pushes the balloon along the cord. A jet engine draws in air at the front. Burning liquid fuel heats the air which is forced out at the back. It is the force of the air streaming out that pushes the plane or vehicle forward. The air which rushes backwards through the neck of the balloon thrusts it forward in a way similar to that of a jet engine.

BALLOON RACER

You will need • your Funstation vehicle • the round balloon • a short piece of plastic pipe • sticky tape • a rubber band

1 Attach a short piece of plastic pipe in the neck of the balloon and secure it with a rubber band.

2 Blow up the balloon through the tube and put your finger securely over the end to stop the air from escaping.

3 Get someone to help you fix the balloon with sticky tape to the front of your Funstation vehicle. Make sure the tubing points towards the back of your vehicle. Do not let air escape from the tubing.

4 Put the buggy on a flat surface and let go of the balloon and tube. The force of the released air as it rushes out from the balloon will move your buggy along.

DID YOU KNOW?

The fastest cars in the world are powered by jet engines. They will travel at over 1,000 kph and have been specially designed to compete in world land-speed record-breaking attempts. Achieving these world records is very dangerous and needs years of careful planning to avoid an accident.

BLAST OFF!

When a Space Shuttle is launched it must reach a speed of over 11,000 metres a second in order to leave the Earth's atmosphere. Once in orbit the spacecraft Discovery travels at over 27,000 kilometres an hour.

A rocket works in a similar way to a jet engine except that it has to carry its own supply of oxygen so that it can fly outside the earth's atmosphere where there is no air. The first rockets were made by the Chinese but it was not until the 1950s that space rockets started to be developed.

Each enormous fuel tank is dropped as soon as the fuel in it is used up. The Space Shuttle has three liquid-fuelled rocket engines which together burn 98 tonnes of fuel a minute.

ROCKET POWER

You will need • an empty 500 ml plastic bottle • a cork • pins and paper for streamers • half a cup of vinegar • half a cup of water • a heaped teaspoon of baking powder or sodium bicarbonate • kitchen paper towel

⚠ Do this outside! Have an adult with you.

1 Decorate the cork with paper streamers. Make sure they are firmly attached.

2 Pour half a cup of vinegar into your bottle. Add half a cup of water.

3 Place the bottle on a flat piece of ground away from any buildings.

4 Put the heaped teaspoon of baking powder or sodium bicarbonate into a small piece of kitchen towel and screw it up into a roll.

5 Push this into the bottle and push on the cork. Do not push the cork in too tightly.

6 Now move back some way from the rocket and wait. There may be some delay as the gas has to build up inside the bottle so be patient and do not investigate the rocket too soon!

There will be a sudden loud pop as the cork leaves the bottle.

Remember to do this experiment only when an adult is present.

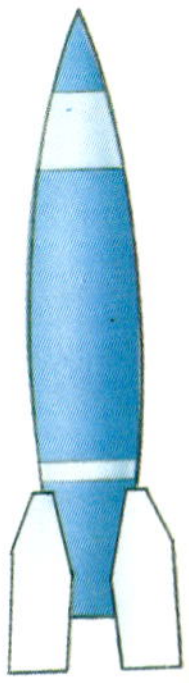

HOW IT WORKS

As the baking powder soaks through the towel it starts to react with the vinegar to produce carbon dioxide. This builds up the pressure inside the bottle until the pressure pushes on the cork causing it to fly out. It is this principle of action and reaction that sends rockets into space.

DID YOU KNOW?

The first woman in space was the Russian astronaut Valentina Tereshkova in 1963 who made 48 trips round the Earth on her space journey. The first man to set foot on the Moon was the American astronaut Neil Armstrong in 1969.

The first space shuttle named Enterprise, made its first test flight in 1977. So far only unmanned space probes have been to Mars but it is hoped that one day scientists may live there to study and find out more about the planet.

CLOCKWORK FUN

Rubber bands can be used in a number of different ways to power toys. They are springy and flexible and have an interesting property called elasticity. When you pull a rubber band, it stretches. When you let it go it returns to its original size.

THE MYSTERIOUS CAN

Rubber band engines are easy to make. This amazing rolling can is interesting to watch and will give you hours of fun.

You will need • a hammer • a nail • an empty tin with a lid • a long rubber band • a large nut

⚠ Get an adult to help you make this. Be careful using the rubber band and the hammer and nail.

1 Get an adult to hammer a nail into the bottom of the can to make two holes. Then make two matching holes in the lid.

2 Cut the rubber band and push an end through one of the two holes in the bottom of the can, and the other end through the other hole. Make sure that you cross the ends inside the can.

3 Tie the nut onto the middle of the rubber band just where the rubber band crosses. Pull the two free ends of the rubber band through the two holes in the lid. Tie the rubber band firmly before you put the lid on the can.

Roll the can away from you and record what happens. The can has a mind of its own!

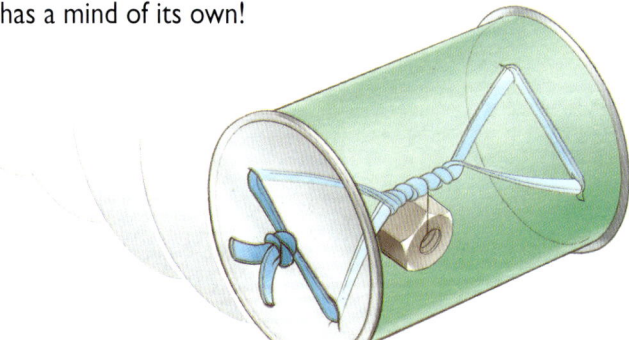

HOW IT WORKS

As the can rolls away from you the rubber bands twist together and are storing up "spring back" energy to use later. When they stop twisting this stored-up energy is used to roll the can back towards you. A watch or a clock works in the same way. When you

wind it up you are storing up the energy for use later. This is called potential energy. After winding your watch, you should not have to wind it again for several days because the stored up energy from the wind-up is used slowly to keep the hands moving .

WHAT NEXT?
• See what happens when you roll your can up or down a slope. Does it make any difference to the way it works?

MAGIC ROUNDABOUT
You will need • a big plastic cotton reel • a dead matchstick or a nail • a short pencil or stick • a rubber band • plasticine • cat and mouse stickers from the back of the book each stuck on card • sticky tape

I Thread a rubber band through the middle of the cotton reel. Thread a dead matchstick or a nail through the loop of the rubber band at the bottom of the reel so the band cannot be pulled out of the top.

2 Thread the dowelling or stick through the rubber band loop at the top.

3 Tape the cat to one end of the dowel rod and the mouse to the other end.

4 Hold the reel and wind up the roundabout by winding the stick round several times. Let go of the stick and watch what happens.

HOW IT WORKS
As it untwists, the rubber band is using up the stored energy that was produced when it was wound up. This is a simple form of the same kind of mechanism that is used in clocks and clockwork toys.

POWER UP!

Batteries make and store electricity. They push electricity along wires and this pushing power is measured in volts. Batteries operate many devices in the home such as radios, toys, torches and clocks.

Inside the dry cell of the battery that powers your torch are three main parts. One end has a negative electrode (—). The other has a positive electrode (+). In between is an electrolyte which is a mixture of chemicals and some cases includes a carbon rod. Chemical reactions cause electrons to flow out of the - electrode into the torch, then back through the + electrode. This power makes the torch light up. As the chemicals get used up the battery gets weaker.

MAKE YOUR OWN BATTERY

You will need • a saucer • scissors • sticky tape • 6 copper coins • warm salty water • 2 wires • wire strippers • buzzer
• aluminium foil • paper kitchen towel

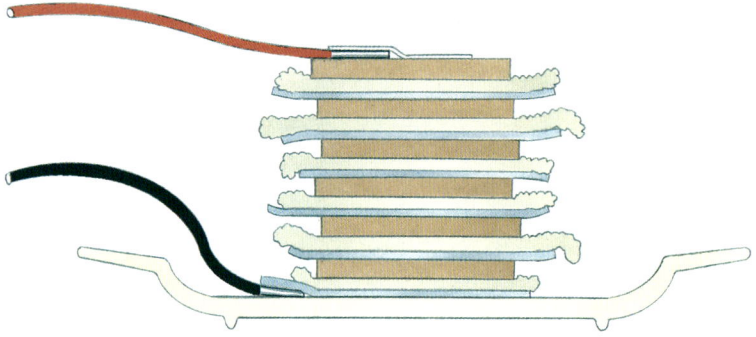

1 Draw and cut out 6 coin-sized foil circles and 6 paper towel ones.

2 Carefully strip the plastic from the ends of the wire with wire strippers. Twist the bare strands together. Tape one wire to a coin. Tape the other wire to a foil circle.

3 Dip a paper towel circle in the warm salty-water solution.

4 Put the foil circle with the wire in a saucer. Put the wet paper circle on top of the foil circle. Place a coin on top.

5 Build up more layers of foil, wet paper and coins. The coin with the wire goes on top. This is your battery.

6 Touch the wires to your buzzer. You should be able to make the buzzer sound faintly.

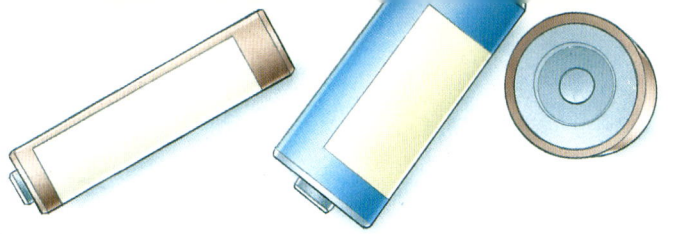

HOW IT WORKS

You have created a battery. When you place aluminium, salt and copper together they make electricity. The chemicals in the pile react together and produce a current which flows along the wires.

INSIDE A BATTERY

The battery case which is made of zinc may be covered with cardboard or plastic. Inside the case are chemicals usually in a paste and in the middle of some batteries there is a carbon rod. As the power is drained from the battery so the chemicals are used up and the battery is unable to produce any more power.

TINGLE-TONGUE TEST

You will need • a piece of copper wire • a paper clip • a lemon

1 Straighten the paper clip and push it into the lemon.

2 Push the piece of copper wire into the lemon close to the paper clip wire.

3 Touch the ends of the copper wire and the paper clip with your tongue. You should get a tingling feeling.

HOW IT WORKS

You have produced a very weak electrical current. The acid in the lemon has reacted with the wires.

ELECTRICAL CIRCUITS

When a battery is connected up current electricity comes from one of its terminals and follows a path called a "circuit" back to the other terminal.

MAKE A CIRCUIT

You will need • 2 AA size 1.5 volt batteries • wire strippers • battery holder • buzzer

1 Carefully strip the plastic from the ends of the four wires with wire strippers. Join the black battery-holder wire to the black buzzer wire by twisting the bare strands of both wires together.

2 Fit the batteries into the battery holder.

3 To make the buzzer sound touch the end of the red battery-holder wire to the end of the red buzzer wire.

OFF AND ON

Fit an on/off switch to your circuit.

You will need • your circuit • aluminium foil • sticky tape • 2 pieces of card about 3cm by 5cm • a small piece of wood about 9cm by 15cm • 1 wire about 25cm long •wire strippers

1 Strip the plastic from the ends of the 25cm wire with wire strippers. Cover the two pieces of card separately with aluminium foil and tape them to the wood as shown, so both cards will touch.

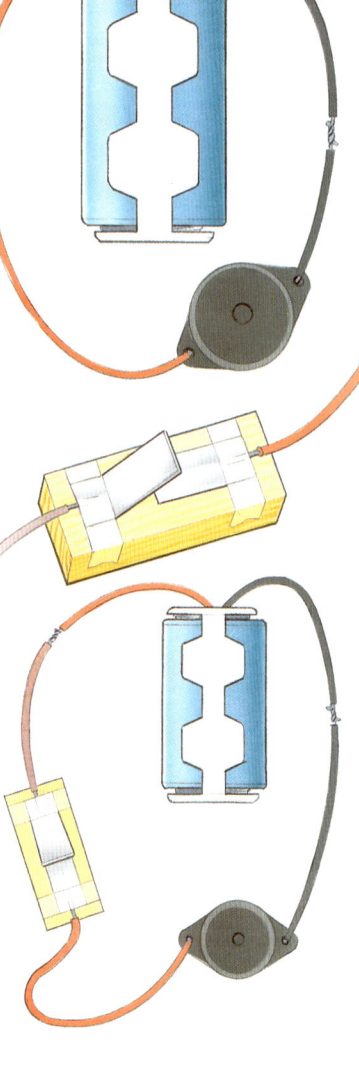

2 Twist the end strands of the red battery-holder wire to the strands of one end of the purple wire, as shown. Tape the other end of the purple wire to a foil-covered card on the wood

4 Tape the red buzzer wire end to the other card as shown.

HOW IT WORKS

When one foil card touches the other it completes the circuit.

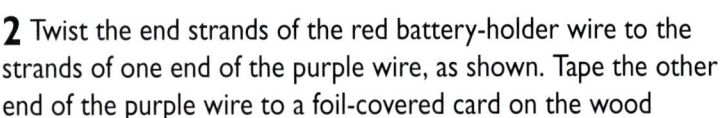

Burglar Alarm

Make your own burglar alarm using the same set up as your Off and On circuit.

You will need • your circuit • 1 wire about 25cm long • 2 aluminium foil strips • sticky tape • wire strippers

1 Strip the plastic from the ends of the 25cm wire with wire strippers.

2 Ensure the black wire from the buzzer is still joined to the black wire on the battery holder, as shown in Make a Circuit, Step 1.

3 Ensure the red battery holder wire is still joined to the purple wire. Remove other end of purple wire from foil card on the wood and fix instead to a foil strip. Fix the strip to the bottom edge of the door.

4 Tape the end of the new 25cm (purple) wire to the other foil strip, then stick the foil strip to the door frame. Make sure part of the foil strip is sticking out and that it touches the other foil strip when the door is opened, but not while it is closed.

5 Remove the red buzzer wire from the foil-covered card and connect the other end of the purple wire to the red buzzer wire by twisting the bare end strands of both wires together.

How It Works

When someone opens the door the two pieces of foil touch and complete the circuit just like the switch in your Off and On circuit. This will sound the buzzer. You could use a torch bulb instead of a buzzer.

What Next?

• Try making an alarm that sounds a buzzer and lights a bulb.

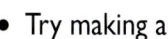

SWITCHED ON

In many houses you can turn an upstairs light off from downstairs or you can switch an outside light on from indoors. Two- and three-way switches are very useful. If you have gone downstairs and forgotten to turn the light off upstairs then a two-way switch will save you the trouble of going back upstairs to switch the light off.

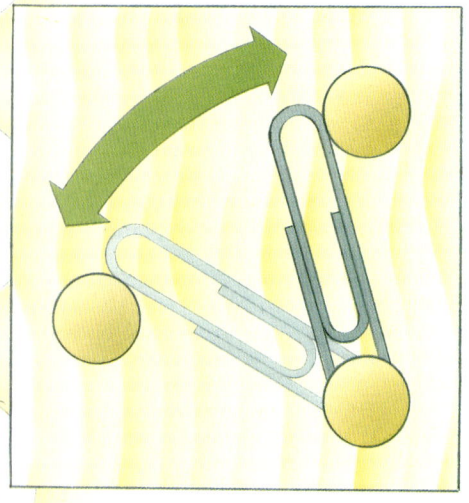

SIMPLE SWITCH

To make your own two-way switch you will first need to make a simple switch.

You will need • a paper clip • a small block of wood • 3 drawing pins

1 Fix one end of the paper clip to the piece of wood with one of the drawing pins.

2 Now push the second drawing pin in near the other end of the paper clip so the clip just touches it.

3 Fix the third pin in opposite the second pin so that the clip touches it when the clip is turned away from touching the second pin. Make sure that you can turn the clip on the first pin and that the clip can touch the second pin. When you turn the clip from the second pin it must be able to touch the third pin.

Use two simple switches to create your own two-way switch.

TWO-WAY SWITCH

Using the diagram below you will be able to wire up your own two-way switch. This will mean that you will be able to operate your buzzer from one of two switches.

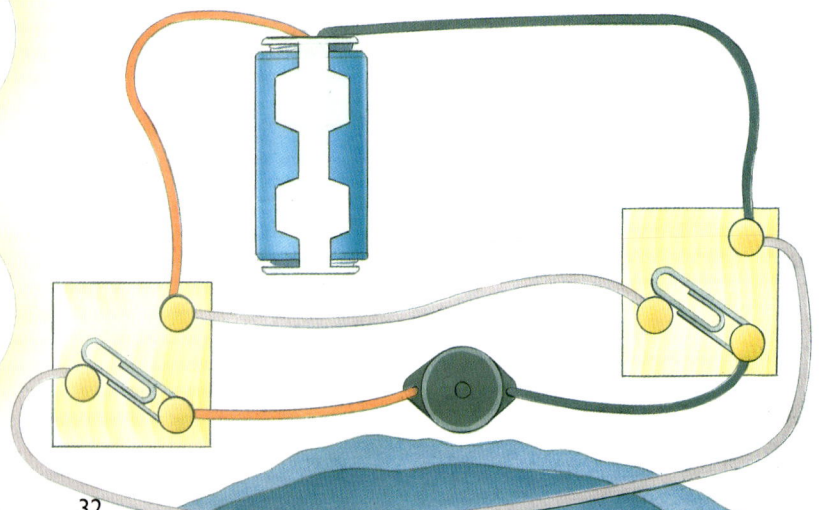

FLASHING LIGHT SWITCH

This can be used if you want to produce a flashing light or an intermittent buzzer. It can be fitted somewhere along your circuit.

You will need • 2 lengths of wire • wire strippers • a paper fastener • aluminium foil • card • sticky tape • scissors

1 Strip the plastic from the ends of a length of wire. Tape one end to a piece of aluminium foil. Do the same with the other wire.

2 Trace round the shape shown here onto card, cut it out and cover it with the aluminium foil.

3 Using a paper fastener fix the shape to the base card making sure that the two ends connect with the two separate pieces of foil to complete the circuit.

4 Turn the circle round and when the ends touch the foil pieces the bulb will light up or the buzzer sound. See if you can work out a way to make your buzzer sound on a regular basis.

WHAT NEXT?

• See if you can produce some of your own switches. Remember that to make the buzzer sound or a bulb light up you must complete the circuit by closing the switch. Opening the switch leaves a gap in the circuit and stops the flow of electricity.

DID YOU KNOW?

In 1937 an electric eel from the Bronx Zoo in New York was recorded as producing 650 volts of electricity which would be enough electricity to kill someone.

Electric eels that live in sea-water do not have to produce as much electricity as fresh-water eels to kill their victims because the salt water they live in conducts electricity better than fresh water.

The electric catfish from Africa is almost as powerful as the electric eel, producing up to 350 volts.

A Secret Code

Can you keep a secret? Being a secret agent is an important job and keeping in touch by code with other agents is vital. Morse code is one of the most important codes used today. It is sent as a combination of dots, dashes and spaces which represent numbers and letters of the alphabet. When a message is sent by sound a dash is a long buzz and a dot a short one and a space is a pause in the sound. A message sent by light is printed as a series of dots, dashes and spaces.

The code was invented by Samuel Morse and his assistant Alexander Bain. In 1844 Morse transmitted the first Morse Code message in the USA.

Secret Agent Communicator

You will be able to make this simple communicator by using some of the ideas you have tried out in the last few pages.

The communicator will let you send Morse code messages to another secret agent using sound or if you are too far away, by light.

You will need • your circuit • thick card or thin wood about 15 cm wide and 20 cm long • thick wood about 15 cm wide and 20 cm long • 2 pieces of wire about 20 cm long • 2 pieces of wire about 30 cm long • a buzzer • a 2.5 volt torch bulb • a bulb holder • a piece of wood • 3 drawing pins • a paper clip • a battery holder • two 1.5 volt AA batteries • nails or panel pins • wire strippers

Stage 1

1 Fix the piece of card onto the wooden base as shown. Use glue or sticky tape or ask an adult to fix it with nails.

2 Fix the bulb holder onto the top of the cardboard using some strong tape or glue. Screw in the bulb.

3 Strip the plastic from the ends of all the wires with wire strippers.

Stage 2

1 Attach a 30cm wire to one of the terminals of the light-bulb holder. Join the other end to the black wire of the buzzer by carefully twisting the bare wires together.

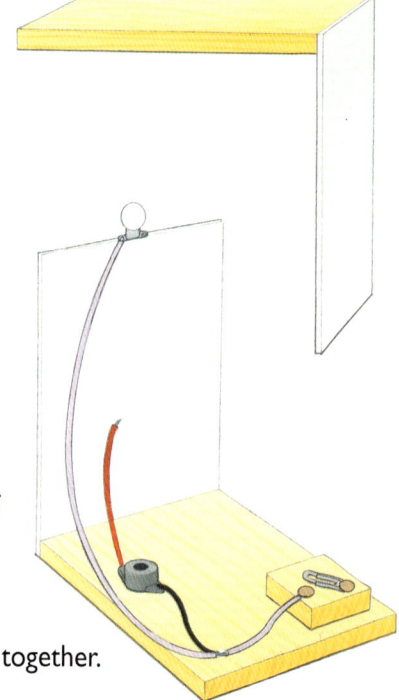

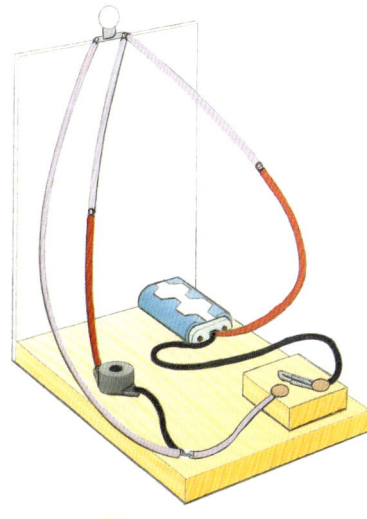

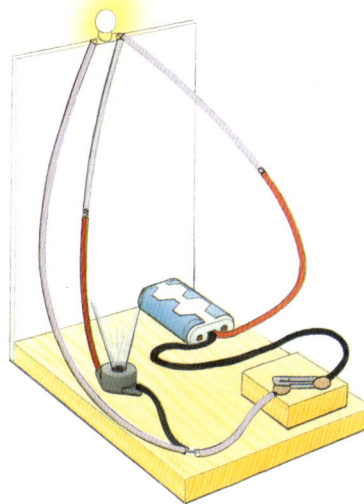

2 Join the end of the 20cm wire to the end of the red buzzer wire by twisting the bare strands of both wires together.

3 Join the end of the 30cm wire to the red battery-holder wire by twisting the strands together.

4 Join the end of the black battery-holder wire to the drawing pin holding the paper clip by twisting the bare strands around the pin.

STAGE 4

When the paper-clip switch touches the drawing pin a connection is made, the circuit is completed so the buzzer will sound and the light will glow.

If you want the battery to last longer leave out either the buzzer or the light when you make up your circuit.

strands together.

2 Attach one end of a 20cm wire to the join where the black buzzer wire and the 30cm wire from the bulb holder meet. Twist the bare strands of all three wires together.

3 Join the other end of the 20cm wire to one of the free drawing pins on the Simple Switch by twisting the bare strands around it.

STAGE 3

1 Attach a 20cm wire and a 30cm wire to the other terminal on the bulb holder.

WIND POWER

Scientists today are looking for new ways of producing electricity as our stocks of oil, coal and gas are used up. The wind is an excellent way of producing power especially as it is free, and will never be in short supply.

MAKE A WINDMILL

You will need • the windmill sail templates from the back of the book • a plastic straw • a bead • a dowelling rod or straight stick • plasticine • scissors • sticky tape • a sewing pin

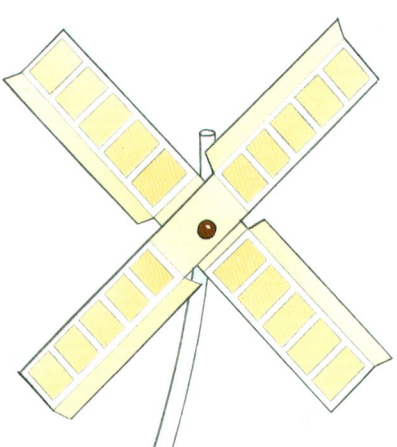

1 Trace the sail templates onto card and cut them out. Score along the dotted lines with scissors and fold along the lines.

2 Put two sails together in the shape of a cross and stick them together in the middle with sticky tape.

3 Pin the sails through the middle, with a bead behind them, to the end of a plastic straw. Insert a dowelling rod or stick into the straw to strengthen it and stop it from bending in the wind.

WHAT NEXT?

• Try your windmill outside. Push your windmill into the ground and watch how the wind makes it spin. See if you can increase the speed at which it rotates by changing the angle of the blades and bending them so that they catch the wind.

DID YOU KNOW

Windmills have been used to pump water and grind corn since ancient times though they were not used in Europe until 800 years ago. Windmills work best facing the wind and one of the problems with the early mills was that if the direction of the wind changed the mill could not move to face it. In 1745 Edmund Lee invented a special fantail which was fitted to the windmill to turn it round to face the wind.

Later windmills were designed so that only the top, where the sails were fitted, turned to face the wind.

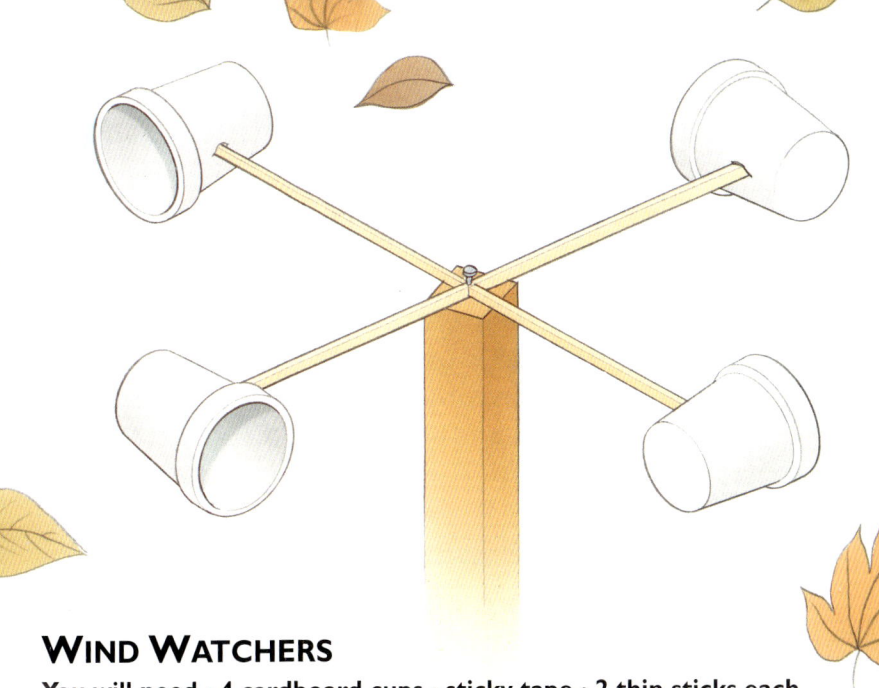

WIND WATCHERS

You will need • 4 cardboard cups • sticky tape • 2 thin sticks each 40 cm long • a nail • a thick stick • scissors

1 Cut a slit in the side of each of the cups. Slide the end of one of the thinner sticks into the cup and fix with a piece of tape. Do the same at the other end making sure that the cup faces the opposite way to the one at the other end.

2 Fix the two other cups onto the other stick in the same way. Form a cross with the two sticks and fix them together.

⚠ **3** Put your wind measurer out in the open, so it will catch the wind. Get an adult to nail your wind measurer to a post with a long nail. Make sure that it can move freely. The stronger the wind the faster it will turn. Record in your notebook how many times it turns in one minute

⚠ TEST THE WIND

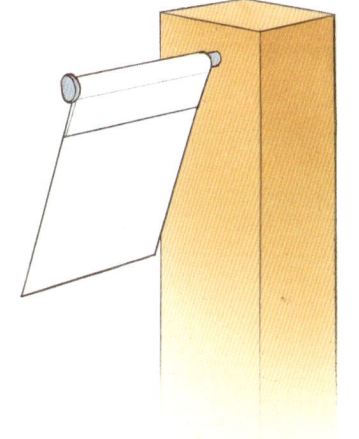

• Use the wind test card from the back of the book. Fit a plastic straw to the top using some strong sticky tape as shown in the illustration. Ask an adult to nail the tile to a post with a long nail. Make sure that the card will move freely. As the wind blows so the card moves upwards.

WHAT NEXT?

• Work out a way of measuring the wind using your wind card or measurer. Record your results.

DID YOU KNOW?

The Beaufort Wind Scale was invented by Admiral Beaufort in 1805. It was originally invented to be used at sea but today it is also used on land.

WATER POWER

Wheels driven by water have been used for centuries to power machinery. Waterwheels were probably first used by millers for grinding corn and today the power of falling water is used to produce hydro-electricity. High up in mountain areas there is plenty of water from rivers and streams to be collected in huge man-made lakes. A dam, built at one end of the lake, stops the water from escaping and it rushes instead down the wall of the dam. The force of this falling water turns giant waterwheels, called water turbines, to produce the electricity.

WATERWHEELS

Overshoot waterwheels are driven by fast flowing water shooting over the top of the wheel. The water falls on the horizontal paddles of the wheel and turns it round. Undershoot wheels are powered by slower water and are often found near the sea. The water flows under the wheel and pushes against the paddles, so turning the water wheel.

MAKE A WATERWHEEL

You will need • 4 blade templates from the back of the book • a cork • 2 long pins or nails • scissors • a large plastic bottle • a plastic tube • a funnel

⚠ **1** Ask an adult to cut four slits in the cork as illustrated.

2 Trace the blade templates onto card, cut them out and firmly push them into the cork. Push a long pin into each end of your cork waterwheel.

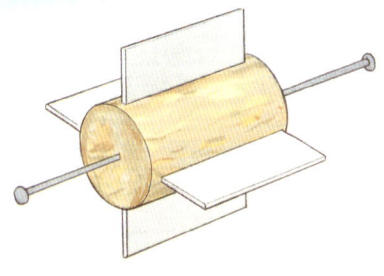

⚠ **3** Cut round the middle of the bottle and use the bottom half.

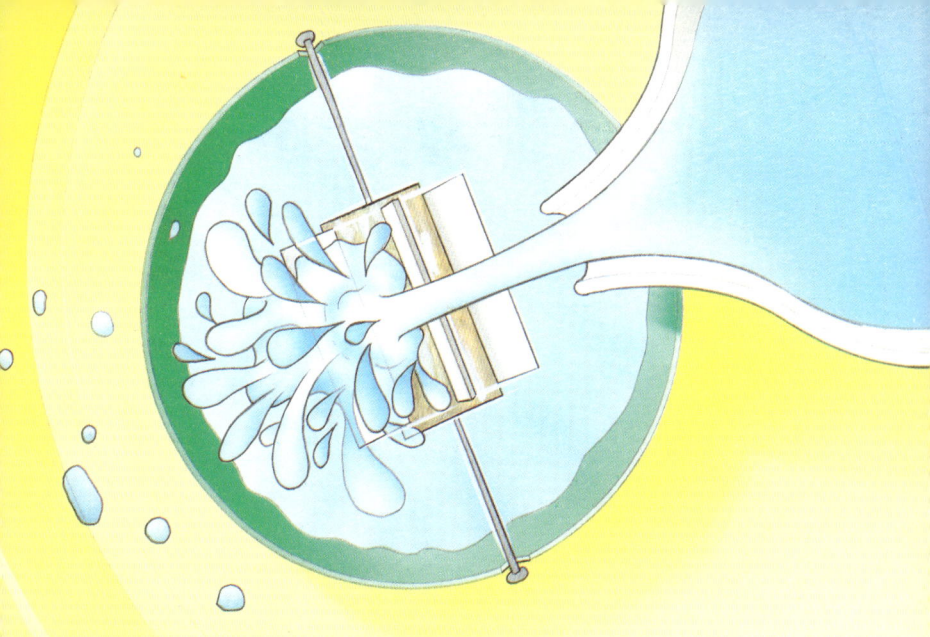

Cut a groove out of the rim of the half bottle on each side to hold the long pins.

4 Position the pins in the two grooves so your waterwheel is placed centrally in the half bottle. Make sure that the wheel will move easily.

5 Fit the plastic tube onto the funnel. Put your water wheel in a big washing up bowl or in the sink. Pour some water down the funnel and direct it so that it flows over the waterwheel.

WHAT NEXT?

• Try directing the tube so that the water falls from much higher. What difference does this make to the speed of the wheel? Record your results.

Fit a simple pulley onto the end of one of the pins and see what you can lift. Are there any other machines you can make using the waterwheel?

DID YOU KNOW?

Turbines were first used about 150 years ago all over Europe and in Central and South America to produce power for factories. Now about one-fifth of the world's energy comes from hydro-electricity. Electricity is measured in units of power called watts. One hydro-electric scheme on the Paraná river between Brazil and Paraguay can produce 13,000 million watts.

UNDER WATER

Submarines travel on the surface of water and by displacing water they are able to dive deep down under water to the bottom of the ocean. They need very thick hulls to withstand the very powerful pressure of the water on them.

Underwater vessels that explore the ocean depths have big tanks that are flooded with water to make the vessel dive.

When the vessel wants to rise to the surface, air is pumped into the tanks to drive out the water, so the vessel will float.

DEEP-SEA DIVER

You will need • a large clear plastic bottle • plasticine • a plastic pen top • a glass of water

1 To make your diver, stick a small lump of plasticine to the tail of the pen top. If there is a hole in the tip, seal it with the plasticine.

2 Put the pen-top diver into a glass of water. Try out the amount of plasticine needed to weight it correctly by adding or removing plasticine until the pen top only just floats. That is, only the tip should be above water.

3 Fill the bottle to the top with water. Put the diver in and screw the top tightly on the bottle.

4 When you squeeze the sides of the bottle the diver goes to the bottom. This is known as a Cartesian Diver after Descartes, the famous 16th century French scientist.

HOW IT WORKS

There is a tiny bubble of air trapped inside the pen top. This is what makes it just float. When you press on the sides of the bottle water enters the pen top so the air bubble gets smaller and no longer supports the pen top so it descends. When you stop pressing the sides water leaves the pen top so the air bubble gets bigger and makes the pen top float again.

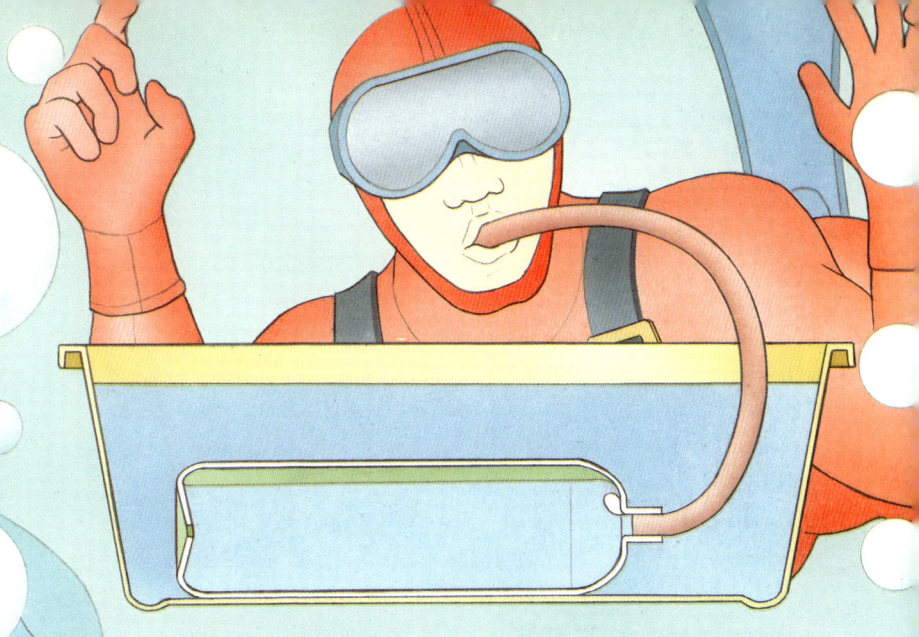

MAKE A SUBMARINE

You will need • an empty clear plastic bottle • a washing-up bowl • a length of plastic tube • scissors • plasticine • waterproof sticky tape

1 Make a small hole in the bottom of the bottle. Fit the tube onto the top of the bottle using some tape or plasticine to seal it.

2 Put the bottle into the water and let it fill with water through the hole in the bottom.

3 Blow down the tube. As the water is pushed out of the bottle it rises to the surface. Stop blowing once it has reached the surface and watch it fill with water and sink.

HOW IT WORKS

When the tanks of a submarine are flooded with water it sinks to the ocean bed. Air is pumped into the tanks to drive out the water. The submarine becomes lighter than the water and rises to the surface to float again.

WHAT NEXT?

• See if you can make some other types of divers using other small objects you can find.

DID YOU KNOW?

The first real submarine used oars! It was built in the 17th century, and was made of wood and covered with a waxy leather. The oars stuck out of the sides of the craft. Do you think the oarsmen would have been very worried about leaks!

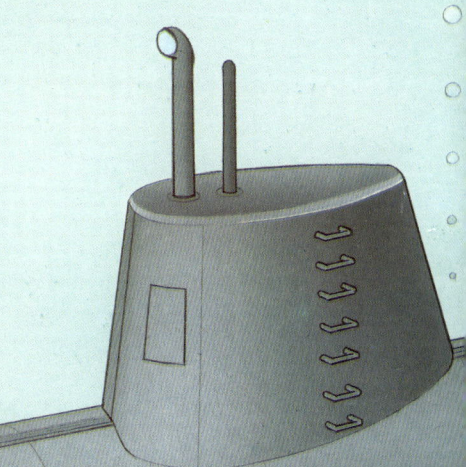

SOLAR POWER

The sun's energy can be converted into electricity inside the tiny solar cells found in solar-powered calculators, radio beacons, telephone links in remote places, space satellites and navigation buoys on the oceans. Solar cells in panels fitted to house roofs warm water-filled pipes during sunshine and the heat is stored to be used when the sun is not shining. Solar cells can also be used to power vehicles but almost constant sunshine and a vast amount of cells are needed. In Australia a solar-powered vehicle race takes place over thousands of miles.

MAKE A MEAL OF IT

⚠ Cook vegetables in a solar-powered cooker. Get an adult to help you with this.

You will need I roll of aluminium foil • a strong cardboard box • thick card • a wire coat hanger • a cork • two paper fasteners • some plasticine • scissors, pencil, glue, ruler • strong sticky tape • 2 tomatoes halved, 4 mushrooms, I small onion quartered

I Cut out the front of the box and make two holes in the sides. Decorate the outside of the box.

2 Cut out a circle of card so that the radius is just less than the depth of the box. Cut the circle in half.

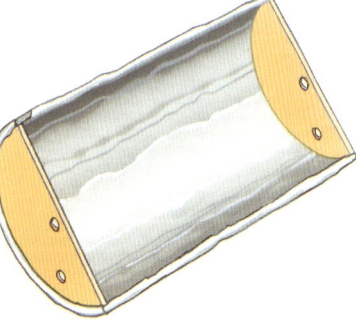

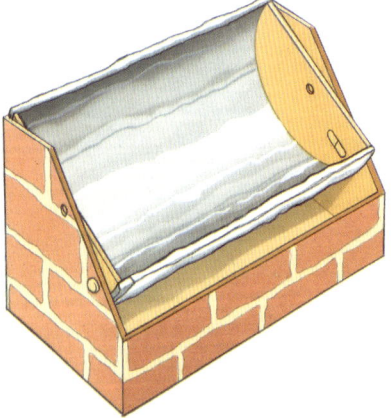

3 Cut out a rectangular piece of card that is just a bit shorter than the length of the box.

Cover it in foil and tape on the two semi-circles of card at each end. This is to be the reflector.

4 Make two holes in each end of the reflector with your scissors, one for the turner and one just below so that it can be fixed onto the box.

5 Rest the reflector on the box and fix it on using the paper fasteners.

6 Ask an adult to help you bend the wire coat hanger into the shape shown.

7 Push the wire through the first hole then through the vegetables and through the second hole. Secure the end with a piece of plasticine. Push a cork onto the wire to be the handle.

WHAT NEXT?

• Take your cooker outside and place it so that it faces the sun. Put some stones into the bottom of your cooker. Make sure you turn the vegetables so they cook on both sides. Record in your notebook how long the vegetables take to cook. See if you can improve the design of your cooker.

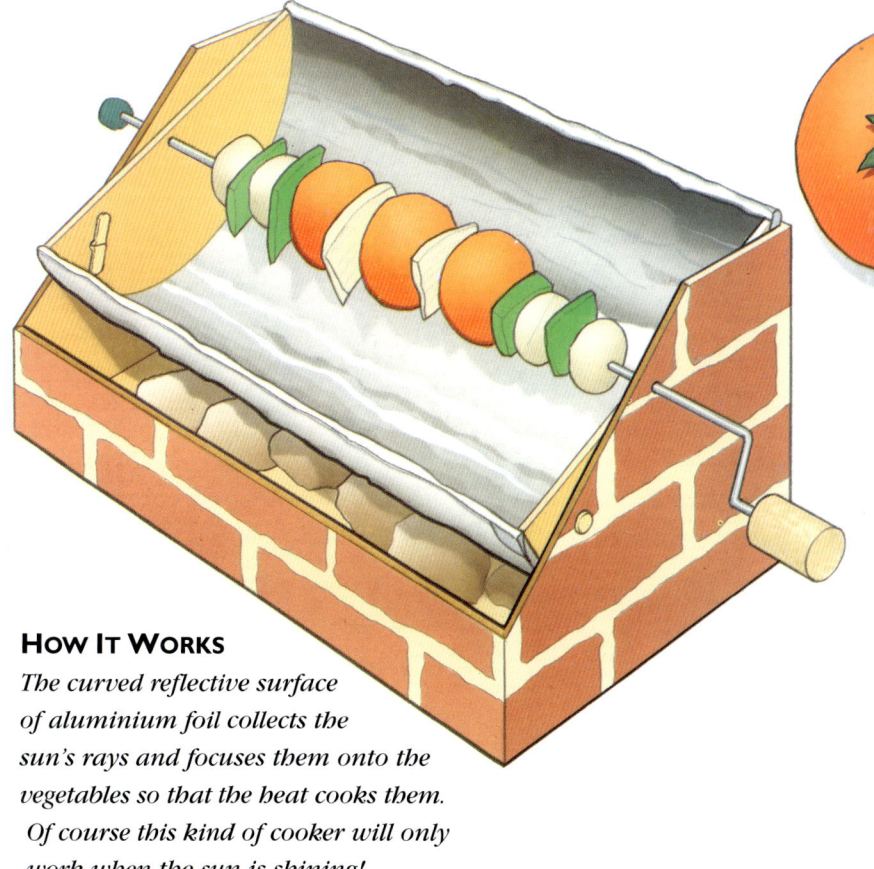

HOW IT WORKS

The curved reflective surface of aluminium foil collects the sun's rays and focuses them onto the vegetables so that the heat cooks them. Of course this kind of cooker will only work when the sun is shining!

DID YOU KNOW?

The solar power station at Odeilo in France has a giant wall of mirrors. These collect the sun's rays and direct them onto a huge tower which contains a boiler. The boiler heats up the water to produce enough steam to turn turbines that then generate electricity.

Hot Air!

Hot air is often used to power balloons. These big balloons have gas burners strapped underneath to produce a blast of hot air that fills the balloon. Once the balloon is inflated it will begin to rise and be carried up into the sky. The balloons are all sorts of shapes and colours and some have advertisements on them. Some look spectacular and are used in special displays and hot-air balloon races.

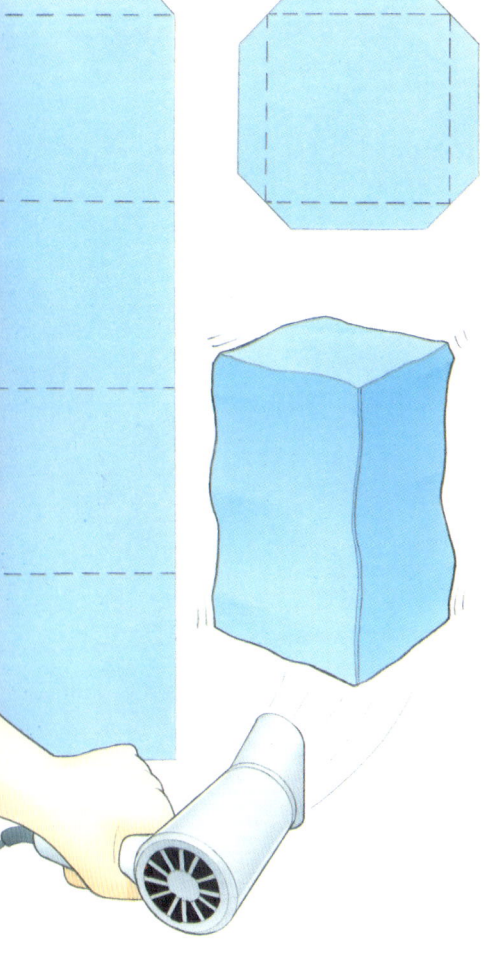

Box Balloon

Here is a simple box-shaped balloon you can make.

You will need • 4 sheets of coloured tissue paper • glue or sticky tape • scissors

1 Cut out a square of tissue paper 8 x 8cm.

2 Cut out four rectangles of tissue paper 8 x 16 cm.

3 Onto each edge of the paper square glue or tape the 8 cm side of a rectangle. The finished shape will be a cross with the square in the middle.

4 Fold each of the rectangles upright and stick the long sides together to form a box shape with an open top.

5 Turn the box over and ask an adult to use a hair dryer on a low setting to blow hot air across and underneath the bottom. Do not blow the air directly into the balloon as the box balloon would be pushed by wind power! As the hot air fills the box balloon it will rise. This is because hot air is lighter than cold air and hot air always rises.

Make A Mobile

Hot air will also make things rotate.

You will need • thread • card • stickers from the back of the book • scissors • a wire coat hanger • strong thin wire 30cm long • 2 pieces of strong thin wire each 15 cm long

1 Attach the four stickers onto your card. Carefully cut around the shapes as shown in the illustration on the right.

2 Cut a small hole in the top of each shape. Tie a length of thread about 6 to 8cm long through each hole, and attach the threads to the short wires as illustrated.

3 Attach the short wire to the long wire with thread.

4 Attach the long wire to the coat hanger. Hang you mobile over a radiator or source of warm air and watch it move round.

IN A WHIRL

In some coal-effect electric fires a bulb makes the fan rotate to produce the flickering effect of real flames.

You will need • thread 20 cm long • thin card • scissors

1 Cut a circle with a radius of 6 cm. Fold the circle in half and then into quarters.

2 Open out the circle and mark along the creases.

3 Cut two-thirds along this line towards the middle. Bend each section of card upwards to make a fan.

4 Make a hole and pass a thread through the centre of the fan. Tie a knot to stop the fan falling off. Hold the thread with the fan on the end above a warm radiator.

HOW IT WORKS

As the heat rises the hot air will spin the fan. If necessary adjust the blades.

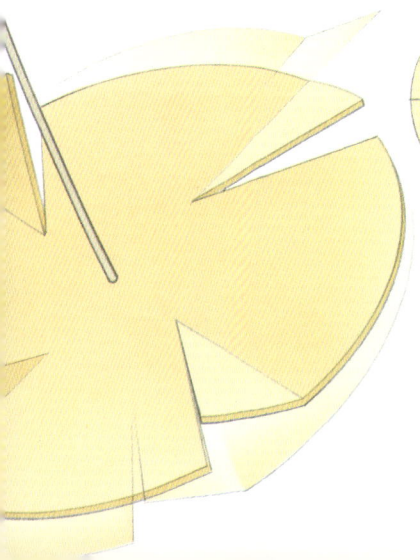

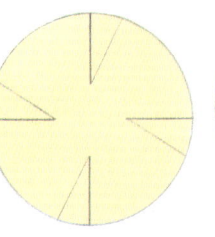

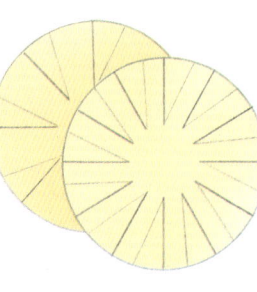

WHAT NEXT?
• Try making a fan with only two blades. Does this spin as easily? Experiment with fans of different sizes.

45

VOLCANOES!

Deep within the Earth there are areas of great heat and turbulence and when pressure builds up enough the eruption bursts through a weak spot in the Earth's crust. Volcanoes can remain quiet for many years before erupting, often with very little warning. The violent explosion of an erupting volcano forms thick clouds of ash and red-hot lava, hot liquid rock called magma, which flow down its sides. The rock builds up into the familiar cone shape of the volcano.

BAKING POWDER VOLCANO

Sometimes when you put two chemicals together you create a reaction. There is often a chemical change and something new is created. This is what happens in this baking soda volcano.

You will need • plasticine • vinegar • baking powder • red food colouring

1 Make a plasticine volcano with a hole in the middle.

2 Fill the centre of your volcano with baking powder. Add red food colouring to the baking powder.

3 Pour a few drops of vinegar into the centre of the volcano and watch the eruption!

HOW IT WORKS

The vinegar and the baking powder produce a fast chemical reaction.

Hot And Cold Eruption

You will need • 2 empty plastic bottles • red food colouring or washable ink • very warm water • cold water • card • a large, plastic washing up bowl • a jug

Do all of this experiment over the washing up bowl and ask someone to help you.

1 Using the jug, fill one bottle with cold water and the other with warm. Add a few drops of the red food colouring to the warm water.

2 Place a piece of card over the bottle containing the cold water. Ask someone to hold the bottle of warm water upright, and keeping the card in place turn the bottle of cold water upside down and place it to touch directly over the upright bottle.

3 Carefully take the card away holding the two bottles in place.

4 Watch what happens. You should see your red warm water volcano in the bottle erupt and rise like smoke into the top bottle.

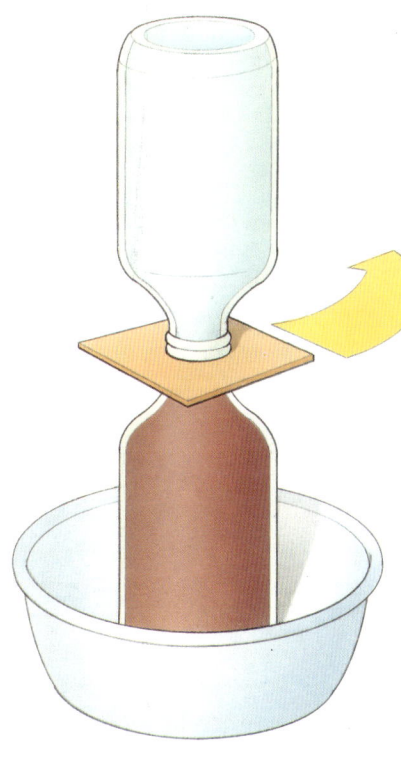

How It Works

Warm water, like warm air rises so the warm red water tries to rise to the surface of the cold water producing an erupting volcano effect that sends up a plume of red "smoke".

DID YOU KNOW?

Of the thirty or so volcanoes that explode every year some last erupted more than 1,000 years ago. Mount Vesuvius, which erupted in AD 79, engulfed the city of Pompeii in hot ash so quickly that over 2,000 people and their animals were killed in their homes. Lava can travel very fast, at speeds over 150 metres a second.

RACING CAR TEMPLATE

Make your car up following the instructions on page 6.

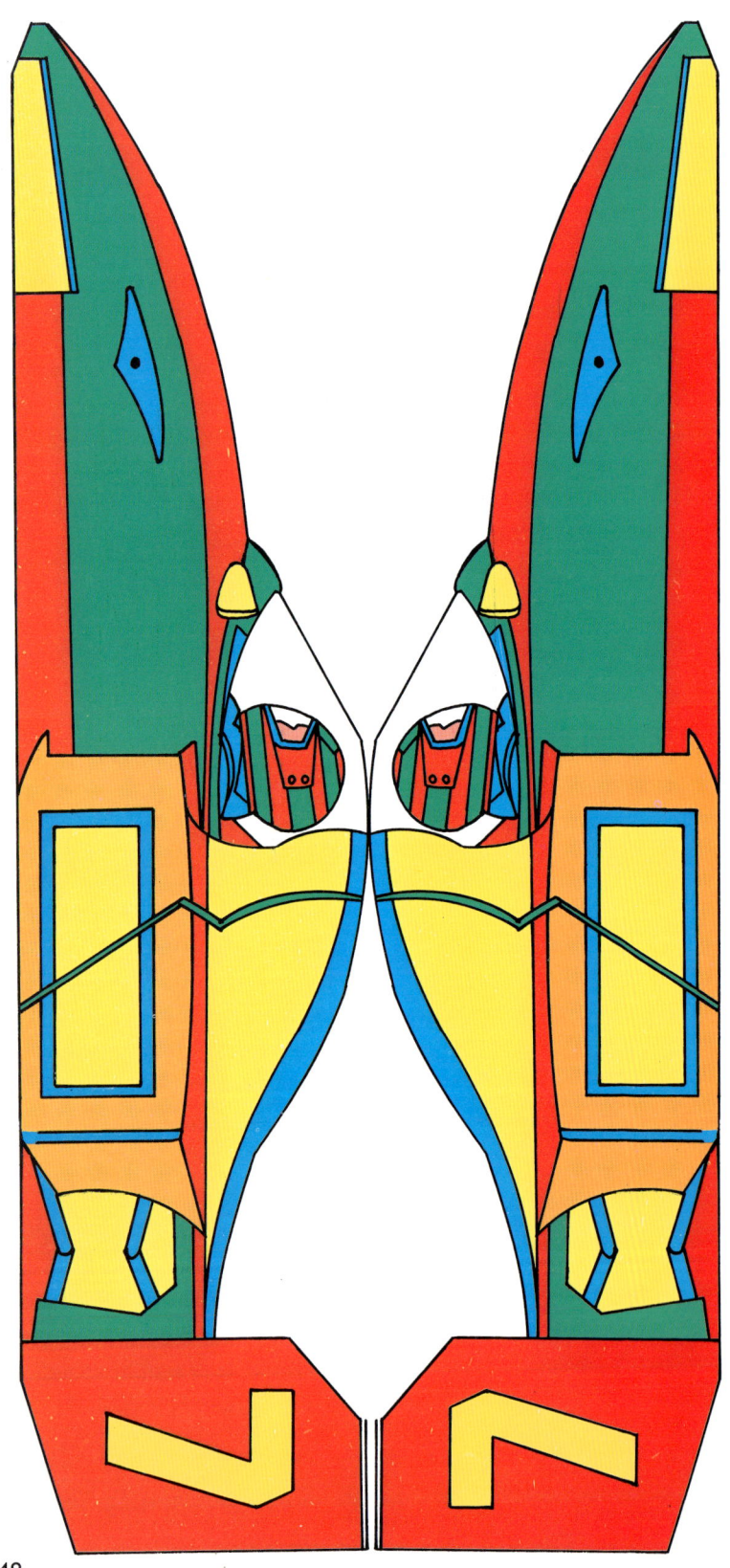

NOTES

Name of Experiment What I think will happen	What I used and what I did	Results

NOTES

Name of Experiment What I think will happen	What I used and what I did	Results
Name of Experiment What I think will happen	What I used and what I did	Results

NOTES

Name of Experiment What I think will happen	What I used and what I did	Results

NOTES

Name of Experiment What I think will happen	What I used and what I did	Results

FUNSTATION VEHICLE INSTRUCTIONS

1 Cut out the seven templates. Score and fold along all the dotted lines.

2 Cut the small cross in the base as shown to fit the straw for the sail.

3 On side 1 fold flap A upwards and stick flap A under shaded area AA on the base. Fold flap B upwards and stick flap B under shaded area BB on the base.

4 On side 2 fold flap C under and stick flap C under shaded area CC on the base. Fold flap D under and stick flap D under shaded area DD on the base.

5 Stick flap E on Side 1 to EE on side 2.

6 On the base carefully push the scissors through the card and cut out the semi-circle for the tube to fit later.

7 Fold up the end flap at right angles to the base along dotted line WX. Stick flap F on side 1 to shaded area FF inside the vehicle base end flap. Stick flap G on side 2 to shaded area GG inside the vehicle base end flap.

8 Fold along line YZ and fold over the top of the vehicle. Stick flap H to shaded area HH, and flap J to shaded area JJ.

9 Cut out the four axle holders and carefully cut the hole in each. Stick the shaded area of each axle flap in place over the shaded areas on your truck.

MAKE A WINDMILL

Use the 2 sail templates on the left and below to make a windmill following the instructions on page 36.

MAKE A WATERWHEEL

Use the four blade templates on the left to make a waterwheel. Instructions can be found on pages 38.

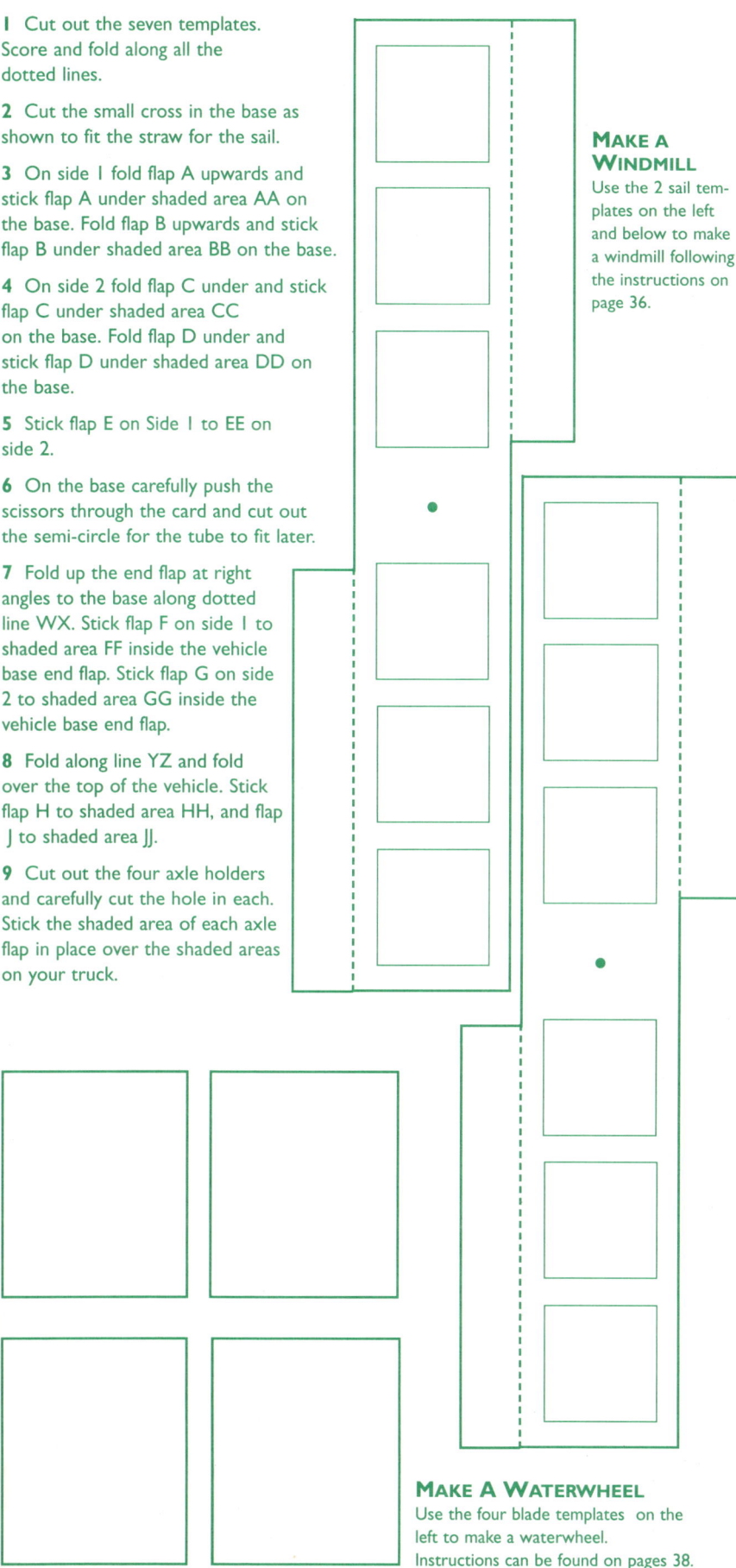

SAIL TEMPLATE

TEST THE WIND CARD

Make the test card below following the instructions on page 37, then decorate it with the leaf stickers.